CHRIS BLACK

I KNOW YOU THINK YOU KNOW IT ALL

ADVICE AND OBSERVATIONS FOR YOU TO STAND APART IN PUBLIC AND ONLINE

powerHouse Books
Brooklyn, NY

INTRODUCTION

Just like Bill Clinton, Jasper Johns, and Gucci Mane, I was born in the South. I always prefer to be in good company.

I had a conspicuously normal upbringing in suburban Atlanta. My mother is a nurse and my father an accountant. Maybe because I've always had the loudest voice in the room, I gravitated to the roar of hardcore punk at an early age. This was the pre-internet DIY era of punk. Information was currency and details were often inaccurate. There was always something to dissect and people didn't hold back their opinions. My fondness for blast beats and breakdowns eventually waned, but my love for bullshitting was just beginning to blossom.

After I realized the "legitimate" music business is stocked with too many people who don't understand music or business, and are especially ill-equipped for the intersection of the two, I slipped into the industry and made it work for me. It was a good run of grass in the green room and cash in the boardroom. And vice versa.

That experience solidified in my mind how similar every situation is and how simple it all can be. Treat everyone the same, look them in the eye, ask about their kids if they have any. If they live in New York and need a guy when they're in LA, give them your dealer's number and let him know they're cool. Always advise anyone against getting a Lambo the first time they get a check that has more than five digits before the decimal point, especially if they have to ask how much the down payment is.

A few years into the music world, I made the move from Atlanta to New York. Everything you ever need is in New York unless you need to have a meeting at Chateau Marmont, and that of course isn't a bad problem to have. Plus that's what Flight 504 is for, right? I eventually branched out from music. When I figured out that I could sell knitting supplies to a luxury car company and advise a household battery brand on how it could raise its profile among tweens and teens, I became certain that a loudmouth with an opinion was a good thing to be. Reality is in short supply.

These days I encounter a lot of people online and in public who all seem to have the same problems. They work in media, fashion, or a fucking coffee shop — it really doesn't matter. They take great pains to deny it, but what they all have in common is they refuse to admit what they don't know. They can't ask questions that might have answers they can't handle and they're terrified to honestly express themselves. The only people who know it all are idiots and assholes. And they're completely delusional. Personally, I like to keep better company than that.

NO. 1
NEVER TAKE YOURSELF TOO SERIOUSLY.

NO. 2
TRY DRUGS, BUT NEVER METH OR HEROIN.

NO. 3
DON'T FEEL LIKE YOU HAVE
TO GO TO COLLEGE.

NO. 4
SOME PEOPLE JUST HAVE LOUDER
INSIDE VOICES.

NO. 5
BE LESS CONCERNED ABOUT GETTING CREDIT
AND MORE CONCERNED WITH THE QUALITY
OF THE WORK.

NO. 6
THERE'S NOTHING WORSE THAN A RICH GUY WHO LOVES NERD CULTURE.

NO. 7
YOU CAN'T HANG POSTERS ON YOUR WALLS AND CALL IT "ARTWORK."

NO. 8
A PLAYOFF BEARD ISN'T GOING TO HELP YOUR TEAM WIN.

NO. 9
WATCHING BASEBALL OR SOCCER ON TV SHOULD BE CONSIDERED A FORM OF TORTURE. HOW DULL IS THE REST OF YOUR LIFE?

NO. 10

ALWAYS HANG OUT WITH PEOPLE MORE TALENTED THAN YOU ARE.

NO. 11

EVERYBODY NEEDS TO MAKE A CONSCIOUS EFFORT TO STOP SAYING "LIKE" ALL THE TIME.

NO. 12

SENDING WORK EMAILS LATE AT NIGHT MAKES YOU SEEM LIKE A CRAZY PERSON.

NO. 13

NO MATTER WHERE YOU ARE, DON'T FORGET WHERE YOU CAME FROM.

NO. 14
"WE" CAN'T BE PREGNANT.
ONLY SHE CAN BE PREGNANT.

NO. 15
DON'T SHOP ANYWHERE YOU WOULDN'T WANT
TO BE SEEN CARRYING THE BAG.

NO. 16
AT LEAST ONCE EVERYONE SHOULD BE THE
PERSON WHO ENDS A TOAST WITH "SORRY."

NO. 17
NO MATTER HOW MUCH MONEY YOU HAVE,
EXOTIC ANIMALS SHOULDN'T BE PETS.

NO. 18
IT'S OK TO LIKE A WHITE FEMALE RAPPER,
BUT UNDERSTAND IT'S A NOVELTY.

"NE
COMPLAI
EXPL
—JOHNN

VER

, NEVER

AIN. "

Y DEPP

NO. 19
IF YOU BREAK PLANS WITH A FRIEND,
DON'T POST A PICTURE
OF WHAT YOU DID INSTEAD.

NO. 20
SOME CAUSES ARE MUCH MORE IMPORTANT
THAN OTHERS SO THINK THOROUGHLY BEFORE
YOU GIVE YOUR MONEY AWAY.

NO. 21
BE AWARE OF HOW YOUR FOOD'S SMELL
MIGHT AFFECT OTHERS WHEN YOU'RE
EATING IN PUBLIC.

NO. 22
BEING RUDE TO THE WAITSTAFF IS AN
INDICATION OF A DEEPER CHARACTER FLAW.

NO. 23
WHEN YOUR DEALER FALLS THROUGH, CALL YOUR OTHER DEALER.

NO. 24
YOUR "OPEN LETTER" FALLS ON DEAF EARS.

NO. 25
MAKING YOUR ONLINE ACCOUNTS PRIVATE DOESN'T MAKE THEM INACCESSIBLE.

NO. 26
PLENTY OF DELICIOUS FOOD IS NEITHER ARTISANAL, ORGANIC, LOCAL, OR SEASONAL, SO JUST EAT IT. YOU'VE MADE IT THIS FAR IN LIFE.

"IF YOU
WITH SO
AND THEY
BOOKS, DON'
— JOHN

GO HOME
MEBODY,
ON'T HAVE
T FUCK 'EM!"
WATERS

NO. 27
WHEN I CALL YOUR OFFICE,
YOUR ASSISTANT SHOULD NOT ASK,
"WHAT IS THIS IN REGARDS TO?"
EITHER GET ON THE PHONE OR CALL ME BACK.

NO. 28
PLAYING GOLF IS A BUSINESS STRATEGY,
NOT A WORKOUT.

NO. 29
HOW SHOCKED CAN YOU BE TO WIN AN AWARD
WHEN YOU KNEW YOU WERE NOMINATED?

NO. 30
YOUR FRIEND WHO BUYS EVERY
"KEEP CALM AND CARRY ON"
ITEM THEY ENCOUNTER NEEDS
AN INTERVENTION.

NO. 31
IT'S NOT CUTE WHEN GIRLS USE THE PHRASE,
"NOM NOM NOM."
IT'S FAR WORSE WHEN GUYS DO.

NO. 32
NEVER CONFRONT
SOMEONE FOR
UNFOLLOWING YOU.

NO. 33
DON'T BE A SLOB, USE A NAPKIN.
LICKING YOUR FINGERS
GROSSES EVERYONE OUT.

NO. 34
IT'S TIME TO RETIRE THE PHRASE
"ELEVATED STREETWEAR."

NO. 35

IF YOU CONSIDER YOURSELF A TRUE FAN OF
MUSIC, SXSW WILL RUIN EVERYTHING YOU
THOUGHT YOU LOVED ABOUT IT.

NO. 36

NO ONE SHOULD
"COACH" YOUR LIFE
FOR YOU.

NO. 37

THE WORLD DOESN'T NEED TO KNOW WHAT
YOU ARE ABOUT TO EAT OR JUST ATE.

NO. 38

YOU SHOULD GO TO A RAVE
ONCE IN YOUR LIFE—BUT ONLY ONCE.

NO. 39
MAGIC CAN BE ENTERTAINING
BUT DON'T LET A MAGICIAN INTO
YOUR FRIEND CIRCLE.

NO. 40
DON'T GET CAUGHT READING A
SELF-HELP BOOK IN PUBLIC.

NO. 41
THERE SHOULDN'T BE ANY ADJECTIVES
IN YOUR INSTAGRAM BIO.

NO. 42
DUNKIN' DONUTS IS GROSS.
IT AND ALL OTHER CHAIN RESTAURANTS
SHOULD HAVE NO PRESENCE IN YOUR
LIFE IF YOU LIVE IN A CITY.

"EVER

IS PERM

AS LO

IT IS FA

—CARLO

THING
ISSIBLE
NG AS
TASTIC."
MOLLINO

NO. 43
A HENLEY IS JUST A DEEP V-NECK WITH
BUTTONS. NEITHER IS ACCEPTABLE.

NO. 44
COLDPLAY IS THE LEAST COOL BAND
IN THE WORLD.

NO. 45
NO ONE SHOULD EVER SEE YOUR BONG.

NO. 46
DO NOT PICK A TIME PERIOD FROM THE PAST AND GO HEAD-TO-TOE EMULATING ITS STYLES.

NO. 47
IT'S BETTER TO GET YOUR OUT-OF-TOWN
GUEST A HOTEL ROOM THAN HAVE THEM SLEEP
ON YOUR COUCH.

NO. 48
PASSIVE-AGGRESSIVENESS IS THE BEST WAY
TO SOLVE ANY DISPUTE ON A PLANE.

NO. 49
HITTING ON A BOTTLE SERVICE GIRL
IS WORSE THAN HITTING ON A BARTENDER.

NO. 50
CANVAS SHOES SHOULD
NOT COME WITH A DUST BAG.

NO. 51
TAN LINES ARE NOTHING TO BE PROUD OF.

"WHAT MAT

IS HOW Y

THROUGH

—CHARLES

TERS MOST
OU WALK
HE FIRE."
BUKOWSKI

NO. 52
E-READERS WILL NEVER BE BOOKS.

NO. 53
JUST BECAUSE IT'S FRENCH DOESN'T
MEAN IT'S SUPERIOR.

NO. 54
WEARING A SCARF IN THE SUMMER IS SILLY.

NO. 55
HALLOWEEN IS A CHILDREN'S HOLIDAY.
YOU SHOULDN'T BE DRESSING UP
OVER THE AGE OF 21.

NO. 56
WHEN VISITING THE HOME OF YOUR SIGNIFICANT
OTHER'S PARENTS FOR THE FIRST TIME,
TELL THEM THEY HAVE A NICE HOUSE.

NO. 57
LIMIT YOUR USE OF EMOJIS.

NO. 58
DO YOU REALLY NEED STICKERS ON YOUR LAPTOP?

NO. 59
IF YOU HAVE TO ASK THE WAITER
A BUNCH OF QUESTIONS BEFORE ORDERING
YOU NEED TO GET IT TOGETHER.

NO. 60
DON'T USE THROWBACK THURSDAY TO
SHOW EVERYONE HOW ATTRACTIVE AND
SKINNY YOU USED TO BE.
IT ONLY DRAWS MORE ATTENTION TO HOW
DIFFERENT YOU LOOK NOW.

"WE'R
ALL SU
TO THINI
—CHARLES

E NOT
PPOSED
ALIKE."
BARKLEY

NO. 61
NEVER GET A LOGO TATTOOED ON YOUR BODY.

NO. 62
GUYS, WHEN YOU'RE HAVING A GIRL
OVER, HAVE AN EXPENSIVE CANDLE
BURNING. THOSE FROM BED BATH &
BEYOND DON'T COUNT.

NO. 63
IF YOU'RE GOING TO DO COKE IN THE
BATHROOM, DO IT ALONE.
TWO AT A TIME IS TOO OBVIOUS.

NO. 64
EVERYTHING IS WORSE IN LAS VEGAS.

NO. 65
NEVER PLAY PITBULL AT YOUR PARTY.

NO. 66
IF YOU REALLY CARE WHAT DAFT PUNK
LOOKS LIKE WITHOUT THE HELMETS, YOU'RE
FOCUSING ON THE WRONG THING.

NO. 67
MANY THINGS ARE JUST BAD.
THERE DOESN'T NEED TO BE A THINK PIECE
TRYING TO PROVE OTHERWISE.

NO. 68

IT'S NOT A COMPETITION;
YOU DON'T HAVE TO ONE-UP
EVERY STORY YOU HEAR.

NO. 69
YOU DON'T LOOK COOL IN A CYCLING CAP.

NO. 70
TRY EVERY FITNESS TREND ONCE BUT DON'T
BUY OR WEAR THE LOGOED APPAREL.

NO. 71
YOU ARE AN IDIOT IF YOU USE THE
TERM "AMAZEBALLS."

NO. 72
HAVING TO TELL PEOPLE YOU'RE AN
ADULT IS A SIGN YOU MIGHT NOT BE.

NO. 73
THAT YOLO JOKE ISN'T FUNNY ANYMORE.

NO. 74
DO YOUR BEST TO AVOID
INSPIRATIONAL WORDS FROM
RAPPERS ON TWITTER.

NO. 75
ONLY DO KARAOKE IN A SMALL ROOM WITH PEOPLE YOU KNOW.

NO. 76
"STREET STYLE" PHOTOS SHOULD NOT COME FROM A MUSIC FESTIVAL.

NO. 77

IF YOU'RE IN COUPLE'S THERAPY AND YOU'RE NOT MARRIED, JUST BREAK UP.

NO. 78
LET'S PUT A BAN ON THE TERM "DANCE PARTY"—EVERYONE SOUNDS STUPID USING IT.

"IF A S
HAS N
YOU WO
ME TH
—IGG

TUATION

O USE

N'T SEE

ERE."

POP

NO. 79
A THANK YOU CARD IS ALWAYS NICER THAN A THANK YOU EMAIL.

NO. 80
THERE IS NO SHAME IN SEEING A THERAPIST.

NO. 81
SMOKING IS ONLY COOL IF IT'S WEED OR YOU'RE KATE MOSS.

NO. 82
QUOTING MOVIES DOES NOT MAKE YOU FUNNY.

NO. 83
DESPITE WHAT YOU THINK OF YOGIS, EVERYONE SHOULD TRY YOGA.

NO. 84
DELEGATION IS CRUCIAL TO SUCCESS.

NO. 85
WEARING A CAT SHIRT TELLS PEOPLE TOO MUCH
ABOUT YOU BEFORE YOU EVEN OPEN YOUR MOUTH.

NO. 86
ANY CLUB THAT REQUIRES DRESS SHOES IS NO
PLACE FOR A MAN TO BE DANCING.

NO. 87
BE WARY OF ANYTHING IN ANOTHER
CITY WHERE THE WORD "BROOKLYN"
IS USED IN DESCRIBING IT.

"NOBODY
A DOL
UNDERES
THE TA
THE AMERIC
—P.T.

VER LOST
AR BY
TIMATING
STE OF
AN PUBLIC."
ARNUM

NO. 88
DON'T BE AFRAID TO
SHARE YOUR OPINION.

NO. 89
NOBODY GIVES A SHIT IF YOU HAVE LIMITED
EDITION DESIGNER ACCESSORIES.

NO. 90
IF YOU CALL THE COPS ON
YOUR OWN PARTY, YOU HAVE TO LOOK
SURPRISED WHEN THEY SHOW UP.

NO. 91
IS EVERY PLAYER ISSUED A
GNARLY NECK TATTOO WHEN THEY'RE
DRAFTED INTO THE NBA?

NO. 92
NEVER ASSUME ANYONE IS GAY OR STRAIGHT.

NO. 93
IF YOU EXPERIENCE SUCH BAD SERVICE THAT
YOU THINK, "I COULD DO THEIR JOB BETTER,"
GET UP AND LEAVE.

NO. 94
YOU SHOULD FEEL GUILTY IF YOU DON'T WASH
YOUR HANDS AFTER USING THE RESTROOM.

NO. 95
HOW CAN I MAKE FUN OF YOU IF YOUR
INSTAGRAM IS SET TO PRIVATE?

NO. 96
DO YOU ANNOUNCE VIA FACEBOOK THAT YOU
BOOKED A TRIP? PLEASE STOP.

"IT'S NOT
WITH PEOP
FAMOUS BUT N
THE T
IS THE F
—RICK

FUN TO BE
E WHO ARE
OT TALENTED.
ALENT
N PART."
RUBIN

NO. 97
REALLY, DON'T TEXT AND DRIVE.

NO. 98
WHEN IN DOUBT, CLEAR YOUR
BROWSER HISTORY AND CACHE.

NO. 99
VAPORIZERS SHOULD BE USED
FOR WEED ONLY.

NO. 100
NEVER ASK TO TRADE
AN AISLE SEAT FOR A WINDOW SEAT.

NO. 101
BOARDSHORTS ARE NOT APPROPRIATE
GYM ATTIRE.

IF YOU'RE NEARING 30, YOU SHOULDN'T HAVE ROOMMATES.

NO. 103
PLEASE, NO MORE VIDEOS OF GUYS SKATEBOARDING IN SUITS AND/OR DRESS SHOES.

NO. 104
WHEN A CHILD IS CRYING ON A PLANE, KNOW THE PARENTS HATE IT JUST AS MUCH AS YOU DO.

NO. 105
GOING TO MUSEUMS AND GALLERIES IS MORE IMPORTANT THAN GOING TO BARS AND CLUBS.

NO. 106
DO NOT HAVE THE TONGUE OF THE HIGH TOPS
OUTSIDE OF YOUR JEANS.

NO. 107
DRESSING UP IN COSTUME TO GO
SEE A MOVIE LETS EVERYONE KNOW
YOU'RE A MANIAC.

NO. 108
REMEMBER THAT PROFESSIONAL
ATHLETES ARE OVERPAID TO PLAY A
GAME FOR A LIVING. THEY SHOULDN'T
BE GIVEN GOD-LIKE STATUS.

NO. 109
CURRENTLY LISTENING ON SPOTIFY TO
I DON'T CARE BY FUCK YOU.

NO. 110
NO ONE EVER REALLY "WINS" BAR TRIVIA.

NO. 111
JUST BECAUSE YOU'RE GETTING A DEAL
DOESN'T MEAN YOU SHOULD BUY IT.

NO. 112
WHEN IN DOUBT, OVER-TIP.

NO. 113
DON'T EXPECT ANYONE WHO HAS SEEN YOU
PLAY VIDEO GAMES WITH A HEADSET ON TO
EVER HAVE SEX WITH YOU.

NO. 114
THE MORE BRACELETS ON A MAN'S ARM,
THE LESS CONFIDENT HE IS.

"BEING FEARL[ESS]
ARMS YOU TO B[E]
IN DOING SO, Y[OU]
THE CULTURE AN[D]
FOR A
CHANGE LI[KE]
—MALCOL[M]

SS OF FAILURE
EAK THE RULES.
U MAY CHANGE
 JUST POSSIBLY,
OMENT,
E ITSELF."
 MCLAREN

NO. 115

CHANCES ARE YOU'RE NOT THAT BUSY.

NO. 116

STOP MAKING PLANS WITH YOUR FRIENDS OVER TWITTER. THAT'S WHAT WE HAVE PHONE CALLS, TEXTING, EMAILS, AND SMOKE SIGNALS FOR.

NO. 117

TAKING A PICTURE WITH A COP ISN'T THAT FUNNY.

NO. 118

IF YOUR FRIEND'S BREATH SMELLS BAD, OFFER THEM A SOLUTION. YOU'D WANT TO KNOW.

NO. 119
IMAGINE A WORLD WITH NO
FACEBOOK BIRTHDAY WALL POSTS.

NO. 120
REALIZE SOME GIRLS ARE ONLY TALKING TO
YOU FOR A FREE DRINK.

NO. 121
STRIVE TO BE THE KIND OF PERSON WHO HAS
A BLUNT ROLLER ON SALARY.

NO. 122
SOMEONE SHOULD TELL THESE RAPPERS
THAT WEARING MICHAEL KORS IS NOTHING
TO BE PROUD OF.

NO. 123
COMMON SENSE IS NOT IN A TEXTBOOK.

"GOOD J

COMES FROM

AND A LO

COMES FROM E

– WILL

UDGMENT
EXPERIENCE,
OF THAT
D JUDGMENT."
OGERS

NO. 124
I WILL NEVER UNDERSTAND PEOPLE
WHO GO TO SBARRO OR JAMBA JUICE IN NEW
YORK. BETTER OPTIONS ARE LITERALLY
ON EVERY CORNER.

NO. 125
DON'T BE THE PERSON WHO WRITES YELP
REVIEWS LIKE IT'S THEIR JOB.

NO. 126
NO MATTER HOW MUCH MONEY YOU HAVE NOW,
GET A PRENUP.

NO. 127
BEING MEAN ISN'T GOING TO GET YOU LAID.

NO. 128
TENNIS IS THE THINKING MAN'S SPORT.

NO. 129
IF YOU'RE GOING TO WEAR A BAND SHIRT, AT
LEAST KNOW SOMETHING ABOUT THE BAND.

NO. 130
GETTING A PERFECT PARALLEL PARK ON THE
FIRST TRY IS A BOSS MOVE.

NO. 131
DON'T RETWEET
YOUR MOM.

NO. 132
INDEPENDENT BOOKSTORES WOULD SURVIVE IF
THEY STOPPED EMPLOYING TOTAL ASSHOLES.

NO. 133
DON'T WORK FOR FREE.

NO. 134

IT'S OK TO WATCH REALITY TV,
JUST BE CAREFUL
WHO YOU DISCUSS IT WITH.

NO. 135

THE PUBLIC ARMREST IS A SHARED SPACE.

NO. 136

THE AFFECTED SHIRT TUCK ISN'T
WORKING FOR YOU.

NO. 137

WHEN THE CHILDREN COME ALONG THE FACIAL
PIERCINGS SHOULD COME OUT.

NO. 138

IF I CAN SEE YOUR NIPPLE, YOUR SHIRT ISN'T
THICK ENOUGH OR BUTTONED HIGH ENOUGH.

NO. 139
A WATER BOTTLE SHOULD NEVER BE
FILLED IN A PUBLIC RESTROOM.

NO. 140
YOUR FRIEND'S BARBER DID A GREAT JOB ON
HIS HAIR. DOESN'T MEAN HE WILL ON YOURS.

NO. 141

ANY WEDDING WORTH ATTENDING HAS AN OPEN BAR.

NO. 142
EVERYONE IS ONE
PLASTIC SURGERY PROCEDURE AWAY
FROM LOOKING LIKE A MONSTER.

"WHEN YOU'RE
WITH SU
YOU CA
WITH COMPLE
—LARR

OT CONCERNED
CEEDING,
I WORK
TE FREEDOM."
DAVID

NO. 143
NO ONE YOU'RE NOT PAYING CARES ABOUT
YOUR DREAMS OR DRUG EXPERIENCES.

NO. 144
AMERICANS WHO ARE FANS OF SOCCER ARE
HIGHLY ANNOYING. ESPECIALLY WHEN THEY
CALL IT FOOTBALL.

NO. 145
IF YOUR WAITER SAYS,
"HAVE YOU DINED WITH US BEFORE?
BECAUSE WE DO THINGS A LITTLE
DIFFERENTLY HERE..."
GET UP AND WALK OUT.

NO. 146
WHEN YOU HAVE THE CHANCE, HOLD A STACK
OF MONEY LIKE IT'S A CELL PHONE.

NO. 147
YOU SHOULD TRY DOING DRUGS AND GETTING
LAID INSTEAD OF POSTING PHOTOS ON TUMBLR
OF CLOTHES YOU CAN'T AFFORD.

NO. 148
WHEN INVITED ONTO A PRIVATE JET, YOU GO. IT DOESN'T MATTER WHERE.

NO. 149
NBA PLAYERS ARE NOT STYLE ICONS.

NO. 150
RESPONDING WITH A MEME CAN BE FUNNY,
JUST BE SURE TO
CHOOSE THE RECIPIENT CAREFULLY.

"ONE MUST
A LITTLE BI
EVEN IN T
OF WI
—HENRY DAV

MAINTAIN
OF SUMMER,
HE MIDDLE
ITER."
ID THOREAU

NO. 151
SOMETIMES IT'S OK TO SEE THE RED FLAGS
IN A RELATIONSHIP AND ROLL WITH IT FOR
A WHILE OUT OF AMUSEMENT—JUST DON'T
STICK AROUND FOR TOO LONG.

NO. 152
A FOOD TRUCK IS NO PLACE
FOR A FIRST DATE.

NO. 153
TAKE "BARKEEP" OUT OF YOUR VOCABULARY.

NO. 154
JUST BECAUSE ONE APPEARS ON
A TV SHOW OR IN A MOVIE DOES NOT
MAKE THEM A CELEBRITY.

NO. 155
EVEN IF YOU'RE NOT A BIG DRINKER,
EVERYONE SHOULD GET DRUNK AT A WEDDING.

NO. 156
THERE'S NO SHAME IN GOING TO THE MALL.

NO. 157
"RISE AND GRIND" DOESN'T MAKE ME
THINK YOU'RE WORKING HARD, IT MAKES ME
THINK YOU'RE A MORON.

NO. 158
NEVER FACETIME IN PUBLIC.

NO. 159
TO SEE WHAT AMERICA IS TRULY LIKE
YOU HAVE TO WATCH *THE BACHELOR* AND *COPS*.
LOS ANGELES AND NEW YORK ARE NOT REAL.

NO. 160
DON'T EVER SAY, "ONE LOVE."

NO. 161
LIKE WHAT YOU LIKE;
YOU DON'T HAVE
TO CALL IT A
"GUILTY PLEASURE."

NO. 162
DON'T FRIEND-REQUEST A PERSON YOU'VE ONLY MET ONCE.

NO. 163
UNLESS YOU'RE FAMOUS, TAKE YOUR SUNGLASSES OFF IN THE AIRPORT.

NO. 164
DON'T ANNOUNCE A DIRECT MESSAGE;
THE WHOLE POINT IS THAT IT'S PRIVATE.

NO. 165
WRITING "FASHION WEEK FUEL"
UNDER ANOTHER BORING FOOD PICTURE DOES
NOT MAKE IT INTERESTING.

NO. 166
DON'T DO ANYTHING REMOTELY
IMPORTANT ONLINE WHEN YOU'RE DRUNK.

NO. 167
MOST PEOPLE DON'T LOOK LIKE THEIR
ONLINE PICTURES.

NO. 168
YOU DON'T "RUN THIS TOWN."

"WHY T
CAN'T I
ALL THE
— KATI

IE FUCK

AVE FUN

TIME?"

MOSS

NO. 169
NEVER BUY THE KNOCK-OFF VERSION
OF ANYTHING. EITHER GET THE REAL
THING OR GO WITHOUT.

NO. 170
NOTHING IS BETTER THAN A GIRL WHO CAN
ROLL A BLUNT.

NO. 171
FIXED-GEAR BIKE DORK OR COFFEE
CONNOISSEUR? IDEALLY NEITHER, NEVER BOTH.

NO. 172
CEASE USING THE TERM "THRIFTING."

NO. 173
COPS ALWAYS CHECK THE FIFTH POCKET.
HIDE YOUR DRUGS SOMEWHERE ELSE.

NO. 174
NOT EVERYONE CAN BE AN "INFLUENCER."

NO. 175
WHITE MEN SHOULD NEVER BRAID THEIR HAIR.

NO. 176
SETTING UP YOUR ART STUDIO IN A PUBLIC PLACE PROVES YOU ARE NOT A REAL ARTIST.

NO. 177
IF YOU HAVE ACCESS TO A PUBLIC ADDRESS SYSTEM DON'T TRY AND BE A COMEDIAN.

NO. 178
REAL STRIP CLUBS ARE IN ATLANTA.

"I THINK TA
HORRIBLE
LIVING I
DRESS FU
– KARL LA

TTOOS ARE
IT'S LIKE
A PUCCI
LL-TIME."
GERFELD

NO. 179
IF YOU'RE NOT PAID TO WRITE, BE DISCERNING
ABOUT WHO YOU SAY YOU'RE A WRITER TO.

NO. 180
IF YOU CRY WHEN A CONTESTANT GETS
ELIMINATED ON A TV SHOW, YOU HAVE TO
CHECK ON YOURSELF.

NO. 181
CALM DOWN ABOUT SEASONAL DRINKS
LIKE EGGNOG, SANGRIA, PUMPKIN SPICE
LATTES, AND ALL OTHERS.

NO. 182
IF YOU REALLY CARE ABOUT YOUR FANTASY
SPORTS TEAM AND DON'T HAVE ANY MONEY ON
THE LINE, YOU MIGHT AS WELL BE PLAYING
DUNGEONS & DRAGONS.

NO. 183

MOVING TO A NEW CITY WON'T
SOLVE YOUR PROBLEMS.

NO. 184

HITTING ON THE BARTENDER AT THE AIRPORT
IS NEVER GOING TO WORK OUT.

NO. 185

DO NOT BUY YOUR DRUGS
ON THE INTERNET.

NO. 186

KNOW YOUR AUDIENCE BEFORE YOU MAKE
DATED REFERENCES.

NO. 187

NEVER HAVE FAITH IN A CAB DRIVER.

NO. 188
THE MICROPHONE IS LOUD ENOUGH, YOU DON'T
HAVE TO YELL INTO IT.

NO. 189
UNLESS YOU'RE IN THE HOSPITAL, YOU
SHOULDN'T BE EATING IN A BED.

NO. 190
WHETHER OR NOT YOU CARE ABOUT THE SPORT,
TAKE BOX SEATS WHEN THEY'RE OFFERED.

NO. 191
YOUR FACEBOOK FRIENDS DON'T WANT TO
HEAR YOUR POLITICAL ARGUMENT.

NO. 192
LEARN HOW TO KEEP AN ATTRACTIVE
PLANT ALIVE.

NO. 193
YELLING, "THIS IS AMERICA!" AT A COP ISN'T
GOING TO STOP THEM FROM ARRESTING YOU.

NO. 194

BEING NERVOUS
ON A DATE IS NOT
A VALID EXCUSE TO
GET WASTED.

NO. 195
WHEN IT COMES TO MOVING, HIRE PROFESSIONALS.

NO. 196
IF YOU'RE COMPLAINING ABOUT THE PRICES
AT LE PAIN QUOTIDIEN, MAYBE
NEW YORK ISN'T FOR YOU.

"I'VE DONE
OF THINGS I S
DO AND, O
NOW I'M GLA
—DIANE

ALL KINDS
ID I WOULDN'T
F COURSE,
. THRILLED."
KEATON

NO. 197
LIFE WAS BETTER BEFORE WE
FOUND OUT OUR ENTERTAINERS ARE
A BUNCH OF IDIOTS.

NO. 198
THERE IS NEVER A GOOD REASON TO GET A
MUSICAL NOTE TATTOOED ON YOUR BODY.

NO. 199
OPENING THE WINDOW IS NOT THE
SAME AS AIR CONDITIONING.

NO. 200
IF TONGUE CAN BE
SEEN THE PDA HAS
GONE TOO FAR.

NO. 201
IF YOU COME ACROSS A QUAALUDE,
GET IT NO MATTER THE COST.

NO. 202
EVEN IF YOU ONLY FLY PERIODICALLY, SIGN
UP FOR FREQUENT-FLYER MILES.

NO. 203
THERE IS NEVER A NEED
FOR MUSTACHE WAX.

NO. 204
IF YOU'RE WILLING TO HANG OUT IN THE
BOTTLE SERVICE SECTION AT NIGHTCLUBS,
YOU DESERVE THE BILL.

NO. 205
THE OSCARS IS NO PLACE FOR A KILT.

"YOU'VE GOT
IN WHATEVER Y
MUSIC, PAINT
BOXING, A
—MILE

O HAVE STYLE
U DO—WRITING,
NG, FASHION,
YTHING."

DAVIS

NO. 206

TEXTING A QUESTION MARK AS A FOLLOW-UP ISN'T GOING TO GET YOU AN ANSWER ANY QUICKER.

NO. 207
DON'T GO TO A "WHITE PARTY."

NO. 208
BE CIVIL TO YOUR NEIGHBORS BUT DON'T BEFRIEND THEM. IT'LL MAKE ANY FUTURE COMPLAINT UNCOMFORTABLE.

NO. 209
NOT EVERY PAIR OF BRIGHTLY COLORED SNEAKERS IS COOL.

NO. 210
IF YOU'VE BEEN SWEATING, WARN
SOMEONE BEFORE YOU HUG THEM.

NO. 211
NO SENSE IN COMPLAINING IF YOU
SAID YES TO A FREE TATTOO.

NO. 212
ONLY TALK ABOUT SPORTS WITH PEOPLE YOU
KNOW CARE ABOUT SPORTS.

NO. 213
A ROLLERBLADER AND LONGBOARDER
COLLIDING IS GOD'S WAY OF WINKING
AT THE WORLD.

NO. 214
DON'T CONFUSE MEGALOMANIA WITH GENIUS.

NO. 215

IF YOU REALLY WANT TO EAT SOMEWHERE,
MAKE A RESERVATION.

NO. 216

HARASSING PEOPLE ON THE STREET
FOR SIGNATURES WON'T GET
YOUR PETITION SIGNED.

NO. 217

REGARDLESS OF AGE, SEX, AND SIZE,
YOU SHOULD BE AFRAID OF
A PACK OF ROWDY TEENAGERS.

NO. 218

"I'M REALLY INTO" SHOULD NOT PREFACE
ANYTHING YOU ARE ABOUT TO SAY.

NO. 219
PEOPLE YELLING CONSPIRACY THEORIES ON
THE STREET SHOULD NEVER BE ENGAGED IN
CONVERSATION.

NO. 220
TALK ON THE PHONE
IN PUBLIC
AS LITTLE AS POSSIBLE.

NO. 221
A PERSON WHO SMOKES CIGARETTES
INSIDE THEIR HOME TAKES PRIDE IN THEIR FILTH.

NO. 222
YOU SHOULD BE EMBARRASSED IF YOU CAMP
OUT FOR ANY NEW PRODUCT.

"I TRY TO
WHAT I WAN
WHAT I WOULD
I TRY NOT TO
THE AUDIENC
—SOFIA

UST MAKE
TO MAKE OR
WANT TO SEE.
THINK ABOUT
TOO MUCH."
OPPOLA

NO. 223
IF YOU'RE IN A LIMOUSINE,
YOU BETTER BE GOING TO A PROM.

NO. 224
WHEN YOU FEEL IT'S TIME TO GO,
IT PROBABLY IS. DON'T BE AFRAID
YOU'RE GOING TO MISS OUT ON
SOMETHING—YOU WON'T.

NO. 225

A MAN HAS NO JUSTIFICATION FOR TAKING A SELFIE.

NO. 226
DON'T EVER SAY,"SORRY, I'M NOT SORRY."

NO. 227

GO TO AS MANY PARTIES AS YOU WANT,
BUT NEVER BRING THE PARTY BACK
TO YOUR PLACE.

NO. 228

TAKING A RED-EYE ISN'T WORTH THE MONEY
YOU MIGHT SAVE.

NO. 229

UNLESS YOU'RE A JANITOR, YOUR KEYS
SHOULD NOT BE HANGING FROM YOUR BELT.

NO. 230

MEN DON'T WEAR T-SHIRTS DESIGNED
BY TEENAGERS.

NO. 231

GO TO ONE NASCAR RACE.

"THAT'S
PLACE T
I AIN'T GOD
RUNNIN' FO
—DOLLY

NOT MY
JUDGE.
AND I AIN'T
R OFFICE."
PARTON

NO. 232

THERE ARE FEW THINGS IN THE
WORLD LAMER THAN AN
ONLINE COMMUNITY "MEET UP."

NO. 233

IT'S HARD TO FOLLOW THE WORD
"DUBSTEP" WITH "ARTIST."

NO. 234

USING A TYPEWRITER WILL NEVER BE AS
COOL AS YOU THINK IT IS.

NO. 235

EVERYTHING ISN'T A PHOTO OPPORTUNITY.

NO. 236
BASEBALL PLAYERS HAVE THE ABSOLUTE
WORST TASTE IN JEWELRY.

NO. 237
PHOTOS SHOULD BE IN FOCUS.

NO. 238
I'LL ASK IF I'M INTERESTED
IN THE DEEPER MEANING OF YOURS OR
ANY OTHER ART.

NO. 239
PEOPLE ONLY DO CLEANSES TO LOSE
WEIGHT. YOU CAN'T STARVE YOURSELF
AND FEEL BETTER.

"MY MO
MORE GO
—JACK NI

TO IS:

D TIMES."

CHOLSON

NO. 240
REMEMBER THAT TAILGATING IS JUST
EATING IN A PARKING LOT.

NO. 241
BEING SUPERSTITIOUS
IS A WASTE OF ENERGY.

NO. 242
CARRYING AROUND A CLASSIC NOVEL
WON'T TRICK PEOPLE INTO
THINKING YOU'RE SMART.

NO. 243
HOLIDAYS AREN'T AN EXCUSE TO POST
COMPLAINTS ABOUT YOUR FAMILY.

NO. 244
CORRECTING THE GRAMMAR
OF OTHERS DOESN'T MAKE YOU
SEEM INTELLIGENT,
IT MAKES YOU SEEM LIKE AN ASSHOLE.

NO. 245
UNLESS YOU'RE HANDICAPPED, DON'T BRING A
DOG INSIDE A RESTAURANT.

NO. 246
DON'T TAKE RELATIONSHIP ADVICE FROM
A MAGAZINE ARTICLE.

NO. 247
WHEN YOU GO TO SOMEONE'S HOUSE AND THEY
PREPARE YOU A MEAL, YOU HAVE TO EAT IT.

"I SUC
BY S
WHAT EVE
IS THI
— JOAN

EEDED
YING
YONE ELSE
KING."
RIVERS

NO. 248
MAKE FRIENDS WITH PEOPLE WHO DON'T HAVE THE SAME OPINIONS AS YOU.

NO. 249
BE CAREFUL WHEN EMULATING FAMOUS MUSICIANS. SOME CLOTHES ARE ONLY MADE FOR A STAGE.

NO. 250
WHEN IN AN ELEVATOR DON'T TALK TO ANYONE YOU DON'T KNOW.

NO. 251
"EXILE ON MAIN ST.": PERFECT FOR ANY OCCASION.

NO. 252
"BINGE-WATCHING" IS NOTHING
TO BOAST ABOUT. IT'S NOT A RACE.

NO. 253
LIVE THE DREAM. SPEND MORE ON ROOM
SERVICE THAN YOU DID ON THE ROOM.

NO. 254
SELF-AWARENESS IS AS IMPORTANT AS SKILL.

NO. 255
THINK BEFORE YOU HASHTAG.

NO. 256
THEY'RE NOT "SHORTS"
IF THEY GO BELOW YOUR KNEE.

"IT'S BET
FAMOUS THAI
BECAUSE
UNFAIRLY
—WOOD

"ER TO BE
NOT FAMOUS
YOU GET
AMPERED."
ALLEN

NO. 257
NEVER FORGET:
SOMETIMES NICE ISN'T
ENOUGH.

NO. 258
YOU CAN SET A PILE OF MONEY
ON FIRE OR GO TO LAS VEGAS
AND GAMBLE IT AWAY.

NO. 259
LIFE ESSENTIALS:
AIR, WATER, PIZZA, WEED, INTERNET.

NO. 260
YOU ALREADY FOLLOW SOMEONE, YOU DON'T
HAVE TO FAVORITE EVERYTHING THEY POST.

NO. 261
IF YOU INSIST ON OWNING
A LUXURY SPORTS CAR, ONLY DRIVE IT,
DON'T TALK ABOUT IT.

NO. 262
TRY AND AVOID ANY PART OF
A CITY WHERE THERE ARE HUNGOVER
STUDENTS ROAMING THE STREETS
IN PAJAMA PANTS.

NO. 263
BEING MEAN TO CELEBRITIES
IS ALWAYS FUNNY.

NO. 264
IF YOU HAVE THE MONEY, BUY ART.
IT'S GOOD TO LOOK AT NOW AND
COULD PAY OFF LATER.

NO. 265

FAT RAPPERS WHO NEVER WEAR SHIRTS
SHOULD BE RESPECTED.
WE SHOULD ALL BE SO LUCKY TO HAVE
THAT LEVEL OF SELF-CONFIDENCE.

NO. 266

IMAGINE A WORLD WITHOUT SELFIES.

NO. 267

WHEN TRAVELING, DO YOUR BEST TO EXPERIENCE LOCAL CULTURE.

NO. 268

IF YOU'RE NOT BRITISH, DON'T END YOUR
EMAIL WITH "CHEERS."

NO. 269
IF YOU THINK YOU'RE SURROUNDED BY
"YES MEN," PITCH THEM YOUR WORST IDEA
AND SEE WHAT THEY SAY.

NO. 270
WHILE IT IS VERY POLITICAL,
IT WOULD STILL BE NICE TO SEE
ONE BAD FASHION SHOW REVIEW.
EVERYTHING CAN'T BE GOOD.

NO. 271
IF WE CAN'T STOP KICKSTARTER
ALTOGETHER, LET'S AT LEAST BAN FAMOUS
PEOPLE FROM USING IT.

NO. 272
ALWAYS SEE MOVIES IN THE MORNING TO
AVOID TEENAGERS.

"CREA
TA
COUR
– HENRI

TIVITY
ES
AGE."
MATISSE

NO. 273
YOU KNOW YOU'RE IN THE RIGHT PLACE
WHEN YOU SEE A GUY IN A FULL SUIT
TALKING ON AN EARPIECE WHILE
DRIVING A GOLF CART.

NO. 274
ALWAYS CARRY CASH.

NO. 275
SKATEBOARDING WILL ALWAYS BE COOL.
LONGBOARDING WILL NEVER BE COOL.

NO. 276
REALITY TV ISN'T REAL
BUT THAT DOESN'T MAKE IT
ANY LESS ENTERTAINING.

NO. 277
PLEASE DON'T SAY SHIT LIKE
"DIGITAL LANDSCAPE."

NO. 278
DO YOUR BEST TO NEVER FLY WITH A HANGOVER.

NO. 279
IF YOU'RE STILL BEING A DICK TO YOUR
PARENTS AFTER YOUR TEENAGE YEARS, YOU
NEED TO LET IT GO.

NO. 280
YOU NEED TO BUY A BED FRAME.
PUTTING YOUR MATTRESS ON THE FLOOR
IS UNACCEPTABLE.

NO. 281
ALMOST EVERYTHING IS COOLER IN JAPAN.

"DON
BORIN
UNFORGI
—JAMES

T BE
—IT'S
VABLE."
MARSH

NO. 282

NEVER FISH FOR A COMPLIMENT.

NO. 283
YOU DON'T NEED SO MANY FUCKING
NAPKINS TO CARRY YOUR COLD DRINK WHEN
IT'S HOT OUTSIDE.

NO. 284
THE BILLED BEANIE IS THE UGLIEST PIECE OF
HEADWEAR EVER CREATED.

NO. 285
NO MATTER WHAT,
NEVER DO COCAINE BEFORE A FAMILY EVENT.
SOMEONE WILL KNOW.

NO. 286
BY THE THIRD DATE YOU NEED TO DECIDE
WHETHER OR NOT YOU LIKE SOMEONE.

NO. 287
ALWAYS BLESS YOUR VALET WITH
LEFTOVER MARIJUANA.

NO. 288
GROWTH IS NOT OWNING IKEA FURNITURE.

NO. 289
DON'T GET A SEXUALLY
TRANSMITTED DISEASE.

NO. 290
VISIBLE NOSE HAIR IS INEXCUSABLE AND MAKES
WORTHLESS ANY OF YOUR STYLE CHOICES.

"DON'
THE TRU
A GOOD
—BILL

T LET
TH SPOIL
STORY."
WYMAN

NO. 291

AT THE VERY LEAST, MAKE EYE
CONTACT WITH SOMEONE BEFORE YOU
START DANCING WITH THEM.

NO. 292

DON'T DRIVE A HATCHBACK.

NO. 293

IF YOU HAVE TO
TRAVEL TO FIND YOURSELF,
YOU'RE TRULY LOST.

NO. 294

NO MATTER HOW PASSIONATE YOU ARE, DON'T
DISCUSS RELIGION OR POLITICS WITH PEOPLE
YOU JUST MET.

NO. 295
TAKE A BREAK FROM TALKING ABOUT
WHISKEY AND BOURBON.
WE GET IT—IT'S VERY MANLY
AND SOPHISTICATED.

NO. 296
ONLY JOHNNY DEPP CAN GET AWAY
WITH LOOKING LIKE THAT.

NO. 297
IT'S A GROUP TEXT, NOT A FILIBUSTER.

NO. 298
REMEMBER WHEN LINDSAY LOHAN
PAINTED "FUCK YOU" ON HER NAILS
FOR A COURT APPEARANCE?
THAT WAS SOME SUPERSTAR SHIT.

NO. 299
SOUTH BEACH IS A EUROPEAN
JUNKYARD DURING THE DAYTIME.
IF YOU HAVE TO GO, ONLY BE
THERE AT NIGHT.

NO. 300

NO ONE NEEDS
ALL THE DETAILS
ALL THE TIME.

NO. 301
DON'T ATTRIBUTE SOMEONE'S
PERSONALITY OR BEHAVIOR TO THEIR
ASTROLOGICAL SIGN.

NO. 302
NEVER GET THE CHEAPEST RENTAL CAR.

NO. 303
DON'T ASK FOR ANY ADDRESS YOU COULD
EASILY GOOGLE.

NO. 304
THERE IS A SPECIAL PLACE IN HELL
FOR PEOPLE WHO CLAP WHEN A PLANE LANDS.

NO. 305
IF YOU'RE GOING TO SLEEP WITH
SOMEONE FAMOUS, DO IT FOR THE STORY.

NO. 306
BRUNCH IS A COLOSSAL WASTE
OF TIME AND MONEY.

NO. 307
DON'T BE OVERLY OFFENDED BY A JOKE.
THE PERSON WAS JOKING.

"TASTE A
IS BEYOND
—RALPH

ND STYLE
CLOTHES."
LAUREN

NO. 308

IF YOU HAVE A WHISTLE IN YOUR MOUTH, YOUR
FINGER ON THE BELL, AND A GOPRO ON YOUR
HELMET, MAYBE YOU SHOULDN'T RIDE A BIKE
AS A MEANS OF TRANSPORTATION.

NO. 309

DON'T BE SEEN IN PUBLIC USING AN IPAD
WITH A MOUSE AND KEYBOARD.

NO. 310

IF YOU'RE A "GANGSTER" TYPE,
YOU PROBABLY SHOULDN'T MATCH
YOUR JORDANS TO ANYTHING
FROM AEROPOSTLE OR AMERICAN EAGLE.

NO. 311

OPENING A DOOR FOR A WOMAN GOES
FURTHER THAN YOU THINK.

NO. 312
KNOW THE DIFFERENCE BETWEEN FRIENDS AND COWORKERS.

NO. 313
YOU DON'T HAVE YOUR PRIORITIES STRAIGHT IF YOU'RE SNORTING COCAINE THROUGH A ONE DOLLAR BILL.

NO. 314
IF NEITHER OF YOU TRIES TO INITIATE MORNING SEX THE NIGHT AFTER FIRST SLEEPING TOGETHER, CONSIDER IT OVER.

NO. 315
OH, YOU SURF? I JUST STOPPED LISTENING.

"MAKING MO
AND WO
ART AND GO
IS THE B
—ANDY

NEY IS ART
KING IS
D BUSINESS
ST ART."
WARHOL

NO. 316
CAN YOU EVER REALLY "HIRE"
AN UNPAID INTERN?

NO. 317
WEARING A BEANIE IN 80+ DEGREE
HEAT MAKES IT LOOK LIKE YOU'RE
NEW TO THE WORLD AND DON'T
COMPREHEND TEMPERATURE.

NO. 318

YOU DON'T HAVE TO DRAW ATTENTION TO YOURSELF TO GIVE MONEY TO CHARITY.

NO. 319
EVERYONE IS AN ASSHOLE.

NO. 320
YOUR THANKSGIVING FOOD DOES NOT
PHOTOGRAPH WELL.

NO. 321
FLAVORED VODKA IS ALMOST ALWAYS BAD.

NO. 322
REALLY THINK ABOUT THE BAND NAME YOU
CHOOSE AS YOU'LL BE ASSOCIATED WITH
IT FOREVER. SEE HOOBASTANK, DEADMAU5,
PUDDLE OF MUDD, AND COUNTLESS OTHERS.

NO. 323
PLEASE DON'T HIT ME WITH THE
VISTAPRINT BUSINESS CARDS.

NO. 324
MOST YACHTS ARE JUST FLOATING MOTOR HOMES.

NO. 325

OK, EVERYONE IS A BRAND OR BRANDING
SOMETHING, BUT THE USE OF THE WORD
NEEDS TO BE SCALED WAY BACK.

NO. 326

YOU SHOULD ONLY ENTER A STARBUCKS
TO USE THE RESTROOM.

NO. 327

NO IPAD PHOTOS. EVER.

NO. 328

IF YOU OPT TO DATE ONLINE
YOU HAVE TO BE UPFRONT WITH YOUR
FRIENDS ABOUT HOW YOU MET.

NO. 329
DON'T GET TOO EXCITED OVER A SAMPLE,
TEASER, SNIPPET, OR PREVIEW.

NO. 330
ONE SHOULDN'T ASSUME
THE SOLO DINER NEEDS OR IS LOOKING TO
BE ENGAGED IN CONVERSATION.

NO. 331
USE A NECK PILLOW ON THE PLANE IF YOU
MUST BUT DON'T WEAR IT AROUND THE
AIRPORT LIKE A NECKLACE.

NO. 332
NO ONE WANTS TO BE AROUND THE GUY WHO
REFLEXIVELY HATES EVERYTHING.

"IF YOU
YOU GO
THE VIT
—GEORGE

O DRUGS,
T TO DO
AMINS."
CLINTON

NO. 333
KEEP IN MIND ALL YOUR PICTURES LIVE
ON THE INTERNET FOREVER.

NO. 334
NO MATTER HOW SUBTLE YOU THINK YOUR
COSMETIC SURGERY IS, EVERYONE CAN TELL.

NO. 335

NEVER ASK IF YOU CAN
KISS SOMEONE.

NO. 336
IF YOU KNOW YOUR FRIENDS WERE OUT
PARTYING LAST NIGHT, DON'T BE UPSET
WHEN THEY DON'T ANSWER YOUR CALL
OR TEXT IN THE MORNING.

NO. 337
YOU DON'T HAVE TO BE SUPPORTIVE ALL
THE TIME OF EVERYTHING YOUR FRIENDS DO.
HONESTY IS MORE IMPORTANT.

NO. 338
KNOW IT IS PHYSICALLY POSSIBLE TO DRINK
CRAFT BEER WITHOUT TALKING ABOUT IT.

NO. 339
YOU CAN'T SET OUT TO MAKE SOMETHING
GO "VIRAL." PEOPLE WILL SHARE IT IF
THEY WANT TO.

NO. 340
THINK HOW LUCKY WE SHOULD BE IF ALL THE
CELEBRITIES WHO KEEP THREATENING TO
RETIRE ACTUALLY DID.

"THIN
YOURS
QUESTION A
– TIMOTH

X FOR
LF AND
UTHORITY."
Y LEARY

NO. 341

PEOPLE WILL HAVE ANY OPINION
IF IT MEANS GETTING CLICKS.

NO. 342

NO ONE SHOULD EVER SEE YOU CONSUME A
TALL BOY ENERGY DRINK.

NO. 343

WITH ALL THE WAYS TO COMMUNICATE,
WHY ARE YOU USING FACEBOOK CHAT?

NO. 344

STOP WHINING ABOUT HOW TIRED YOU ARE.

NO. 345

KNOW WHEN TO LOG OFF.

NO. 346

IF YOU ARE WILLING TO
PAY TOP DOLLAR FOR A
BANKSY PRINT, YOU NEED TO
REEVALUATE EVERYTHING.

NO. 347

OUTRAGE IS THE GO-TO EMOTION
FOR AMATEUR CRITICS.

NO. 348

KNOW HOW TO PREPARE
AT LEAST ONE GREAT MEAL (THAT DOESN'T
INVOLVE A MICROWAVE).

NO. 349

ICED COFFEE IS NOT HOT COFFEE
POURED OVER ICE.

"I RE
THE MORE
THE MORE
I WAS V
THE BETTER
–BILL

LIZED
UN I HAD,
RELAXED
ORKING,
I WORKED."
URRAY

NO. 350
IF SETTING YOUR FRIENDS UP
ON A DATE HAS THE POTENTIAL TO BACKFIRE
ON YOUR LIFE, DON'T DO IT.

NO. 351

THE HANGOVER CURE
TRIFECTA: WATER, WEED,
AND XANAX.

NO. 352
WHY ARE YOU USING TUMBLR TO ASK FOR LIFE
ADVICE FROM AN ANONYMOUS PERSON?

NO. 353
YOU CAN'T UNFOLLOW EMAIL.

NO. 354
NO MATTER HOW UNCOOL YOU THINK
IT LOOKS, WEAR EARPLUGS WHEN YOU'RE
AROUND LOUD MUSIC.

NO. 355
CELEBRITIES BEING OBNOXIOUS
IS NOT NEWS.

NO. 356
LISTENING TO RADIOHEAD IN A COFFEE SHOP
IS TOO PREDICTABLE.

NO. 357
A PERSON WHO BOARDS AN AIRPLANE
WITH NO CARRY-ON ITEMS
IS EITHER A SERIAL KILLER OR A GENIUS.
THERE IS NO IN-BETWEEN.

"LIFE HA

IMMEASURABLY

I HAVE BEE

STOP TAKING

—HUNTER S

BECOME
BETTER SINCE
FORCED TO
SERIOUSLY."
THOMPSON

NO. 358
STRIVE TO LIVE A LIFE WITHOUT PUBLIC
LAUNDRY FACILITIES.

NO. 359
POSTING A BABY PHOTO OF YOURSELF IS
AN OBVIOUS CRY FOR ATTENTION.

NO. 360
THERE ARE SO MANY FASCINATING
THINGS IN THIS WORLD. MIXOLOGY
IS NOT ONE OF THEM.

NO. 361
NEVER ASK SOMEONE TO FOLLOW YOU
ON SOCIAL MEDIA.
IF THEY'RE INTERESTED, THEY WILL.

NO. 362
IT'S A SAD DAY WHEN PAGE SIX
RUNS A STORY ABOUT A DJ.

NO. 363
DON'T EVER USE THE WORD "CURATE" WHEN MENTIONING YOUR SOCIAL MEDIA ACCOUNTS.

NO. 364
IF YOU WATCH SINGING
COMPETITION SHOWS, DON'T TELL
PEOPLE THAT YOU WATCH SINGING
COMPETITION SHOWS.

NO. 365
IF SOMEONE TEXTS YOU SOMETHING AND
YOUR INITIAL REACTION IS, "WHO CARES?"
IT'S OK TO RESPOND WITH THAT.

NO. 366
YOU SHOULDN'T REFER TO YOUR
OWN ALBUM, FILM, OR PROJECT AS
"HIGHLY ANTICIPATED."

NO. 367
IT ONLY TAKES ONE CUPCAKE TO WIN
OVER A SORORITY GIRL.

NO. 368
NEVER TAG YOURSELF IN YOUR OWN
INSTAGRAM PICTURE.

NO. 369

BEING A WELL-ROUNDED PERSON WILL GET YOU LAID.

NO. 370
ANYONE POSTING PHOTOS
OF THEMSELVES IN THEIR UNDERWEAR NEEDS
TO HAVE THEIR HEAD CHECKED.

NO. 371
MAINTAIN CONTROL OF YOUR PHONE
WHEN SHOWING SOMEONE PHOTOS.
YOU DON'T WANT THEM
SEEING SOMETHING THEY SHOULDN'T.

"IF IT'S
DO AND Y
IT, THEN Y
—VAN M

/HAT YOU
U CAN DO
OU DO IT."
RRISON

NO. 372
FRENCH PRESS:
THE MOST ANNOYING WAY TO BE SERVED
COFFEE AT A RESTAURANT.

NO. 373
MIXING UPPERS AND DOWNERS
NEVER ENDS WELL.

NO. 374
DON'T MAKE EVERY HOLIDAY
ANOTHER EXCUSE FOR A PROMOTIONAL EMAIL.

NO. 375
HAVING A WELL-FOLLOWED BLOG IS
THE SAME AS BEING THE CAPTAIN OF YOUR
HIGH SCHOOL SPORTS TEAM—PEOPLE DON'T
WANT TO HEAR ABOUT IT.

NO. 376

IT'S PERFECTLY ACCEPTABLE TO ADMIT YOU DON'T KNOW SOMETHING.

NO. 377

PEOPLE WITH EYEBROW PIERCINGS
ARE OBLIVIOUS TO THE WORLD AROUND THEM.

NO. 378

DON'T BRING YOUR DOG ON THE PLANE.

NO. 379

IF ALL YOUR FRIENDS THINK
THE PERSON YOU'RE DATING IS TERRIBLE,
THEY'RE PROBABLY RIGHT.

"GETTING
WITH FRIEND
COURT OVE
ONE (
GREAT THIN
—ROBER

TOGETHER
AND HOLDING
A MEAL IS
F THE
S IN LIFE."
DUVALL

NO. 380
DON'T PUBLICLY HUMILIATE
YOURSELF BY TWEETING AT CELEBRITIES
AND WAITING FOR A RESPONSE.

NO. 381
DON'T LIKE KANYE WEST TOO MUCH.

NO. 382

PIZZA HEALS ALL WOUNDS.

NO. 383
IF YOU'RE GOING TO DE-FRIEND
SOMEONE ON FACEBOOK, DO IT ON THEIR
BIRTHDAY AND THEY'LL NEVER NOTICE.

NO. 384
DON'T BUY YOUR GROCERIES AT WALMART.

NO. 385
YOUR OBNOXIOUS WATERMARK
RUINS YOUR PHOTO.

NO. 386
STOP TRYING TO MAKE FOOTBALL
AND FASHION A THING.

NO. 387
YOU SHOULD SPEND THAT NEW YEAR'S
EVE OUTFIT MONEY ON DRUGS SO YOU
ACTUALLY HAVE FUN ON THE WORST PARTY
NIGHT OF THE YEAR.

NO. 388
DO NOT OWN A WHITE LEATHER SOFA.

NO. 389
BE VERY CAREFUL WITH PREPACKAGED SUSHI.

NO. 390
REMOVE THE WRISTBAND AS SOON
AS THE FESTIVAL IS OVER.
WEARING IT AFTER AS JEWELRY IS
NOT AN OPTION.

NO. 391
BE WARY OF ANY PERSON WHO
CLOTHES THEIR PET.

NO. 392
IF YOU'RE WILLING TO POST
THINGS ONLINE FOR THE WORLD
TO SEE, THEN YOU SHOULDN'T BE AFRAID
OF PUBLIC SPEAKING.

NO. 393
DISABLING ALL COMMENTS SECTIONS WOULD
MAKE THE WORLD A BETTER PLACE.

NO. 394

PEOPLE LOVE TO COMPLAIN
ABOUT THE TSA BUT THEY HAVE THE POWER
TO MAKE SOMEONE REMOVE A FEDORA.
WE SHOULD ALL BE SO LUCKY.

NO. 395

ONLY A DICKHEAD PAYS FOR A SMALL SNACK
OR DRINK WITH A CREDIT CARD.

NO. 396

TRY NOT TO BE OVERLY CONCERNED WITH "NETWORKING." DEFINITELY DON'T THROW THE TERM AROUND.

"NEVER
THE SIZE
PAYCHECK W
OF YOUR
—MARLOI

CONFUSE
OF YOUR
TH THE SIZE
ALENT."
BRANDO

NO. 397
LIMIT THE NUMBER OF PEOPLE
YOU REFER TO AS YOUR "BEST FRIEND."

NO. 398
LADIES, DO NOT PAINT YOUR NAILS
AT THE AIRPORT. YOU CAN'T PUSH THAT SMELL
ON INNOCENT BYSTANDERS.

NO. 399
IF SOMETHING COSTS A LOT OF MONEY THAT DOESN'T MEAN IT'S COOL.

NO. 400
HOW LONG BEFORE HEADPHONES TURN
INTO FULL SIZE HELMETS WITH
ALL-OVER PRINT LOGOS?

NO. 401
HAVING A CLEVER WI-FI NETWORK NAME ISN'T GOING TO GET YOU ANYWHERE.

NO. 402
IF YOU CHOOSE TO WORK IN FASHION, YOU CAN'T REALLY COMPLAIN ABOUT FASHION WEEK.

NO. 403
DON'T CHEAP OUT AND MAKE A LYRIC VIDEO. EITHER MAKE A MUSIC VIDEO OR DON'T.

NO. 404
BEING AFRAID OF GETTING A COMPUTER VIRUS IS SOMETHING RESERVED FOR ONLY YOUR PARENTS.

NO. 405
LOVE YOUR TEAM? A CAP IS SUFFICIENT IN PROCLAIMING IT.

NO. 406
ALWAYS BRING A GIFT TO A PARTY.
IF YOU'RE NOT SURE,
THE ANSWER IS ALWAYS CHAMPAGNE.

NO. 407
JUST BECAUSE YOUR FLIGHT WAS DELAYED
DOESN'T PERMIT YOU TO TAKE YOUR SHOES
OFF IN THE TERMINAL.

NO. 408
NEW YORK IS THE BEST AND WORST OF
EVERYTHING ALL IN ONE PLACE.

NO. 409
WHEN BEING PHOTOGRAPHED REFRAIN
FROM FLASHING THESE HAND GESTURES:
PEACE, HANG LOOSE, HORNS.

NO. 410

TELLING A GIRL TO SMILE IS NOT AN
ACCEPTABLE OPENING LINE.

NO. 411

USE WHAT YOU BUY AND DON'T BE TOO
PRECIOUS ABOUT ANY OF IT.

NO. 412

LOOK FORWARD MUCH MORE OFTEN THAN YOU
LOOK BACKWARD.

NO. 413

IT'S OK TO DENY SOMEONE'S FIST BUMP.

NO. 414

NO ONE LIKES
A KNOW-IT-ALL.

ACKNOWLEDGMENTS

Nikki Jagerman for her humor, assistance, and organization throughout this entire process; Ezra Morris for his creativity and insight; my wife Hayley Phelan for putting up with all of my shit; Wes Del Val and Craig Cohen at powerHouse Books for taking a chance on this concept; Andrew Wren for his design expertise; Amardeep Singh, Dana Veraldi, James Ellis, Jason Stewart, Brad Bennett, Jake Davis, Farshad Arshid, Mike McKoy, Christopher Sullivan, Gary and Lynda Black, Ansley Black, Sour Diesel, Xanax, New York City, Los Angeles, Atlanta, and anyone who has ever listened to me rant and rave or follows me on Twitter.

To anybody that wakes up and strives to do what they want everyday, this is for you.

Chris Black is a writer, producer, and editor living in New York City. His agency, Done to Death Projects, has worked with New Balance, VICE, and Harry's, among other clients. His Twitter feed offers "high level cultural commentary" and is required reading for discriminating members of the publishing, photography, music, filmmaking, fashion, and consulting worlds. Black writes a regular column for Style.com and frequently contributes to Inventory, The World's Best Ever, and Yahoo. His connection to popular culture - whether creating it, critiquing it, or celebrating it - is constantly expanding and new collaborations, farther destinations, and greater inspirations always await.

I Know You Think You Know It All:
Advice and Observations for You to Stand Apart in Public and Online

Text © 2015 Chris Black

Published in the United States by powerHouse
Books,a division of powerHouse Cultural
Entertainment, Inc.

37 Main Street, Brooklyn, NY 11201-1021
Tel 212.604.9074, Fax 212.366.5247
info@powerHouseBooks.com
www.powerHouseBooks.com

First edition, 2015

Library of Congress Control Number: 2014960221

ISBN 978-1-57687-735-7

Printed by: Toppan Leefung Printing Ltd

Design by: Out There

10 9 8 7 6 5 4 3 2

Printed and bound in China

31901056375035